A Perfect Balance

The ultimate guide to professionally balancing food and wine flavours

Foreword

It is a great pleasure for me to write this foreword to Andrew and Janet Coghlan's excellent cookery book. This is however a cookery book with a bit of a difference, in that they have persuaded various friends who are chefs at some of the most outstanding hotels in the UK and Ireland to be involved in guest chapters, the most interesting aspect of which is Andrew's wine matching suggestions that are included in all of them.

It is a beautifully illustrated and produced book, but don't think that it is one just to leave lying about on your coffee table. It is full of helpful suggestions, and many of the wine ideas are certainly new to me and well worth trying out. As wine lists become increasingly international and wine producing more and more sophisticated it is a great boon to have such sensible and intelligent advice as is provided here. It is a relief not to be talked down to by the wine experts, and the understanding that Andrew has for many of the difficult decisions which host and hostesses have to make is particularly welcome.

The sheer pleasure of hospitality shines through this book from the very first page, and whilst some of the professional chefs' creations may be beyond mere mortal cooks, the ideas that they have are well worth trying out.

For me the very best feature of a really good book is the emphasis on local produce; it must make sense for us to buy, cook and eat locally produced food whenever possible. Andrew and Janet have gone out of their way to find reliable local producers and I thoroughly applaud this extremely responsible approach. British farmers and horticulturalists produce high quality products and the more that such quality is understood in the market place the better not only for the consumer but also for the future of farming in the UK.

Devonshire

The Duke of Devonshire CBE

The Duke & Duchess of Devonshire, Chatsworth House, Derbyshire

Dedications

This book is dedicated to our parents, Ellen & Ron Davidson,
Anne & Eddie Coghlan, who have supported us in many different
ways over the years.

Particular credit to Anne Coghlan, the original founder of Wine Schoppen
in 1979. Anne has provided us with a firm foundation to work from.

Special thanks to our head chef Simon Lilley for his hard work and
dedication to Coghlans over the past 15 years, which is much appreciated
but seldom acknowledged and to all the staff of
Coghlans, Barrels and Bottles and Wine Schoppen who work
so hard behind the scenes.

Thank you to all of the Hoteliers and Chefs who have contributed to this
book, whilst striving to achieve excellence in their chosen fields.

Personal thanks extend to the Duke and Duchess of Devonshire for their
support of this project and for their good humour and company during
the Chatsworth International Horse Trials.

For the winemakers who have produced such stunning wines for us to
work with over the years. Their passion shows through in the wines
chosen for this book.

Edited by: *Andy Waple*
Design & Origination: *Paul Cocker*
Contributors: *Martin Edwards*
Photography: *Peter Goulding, f-eleven photography*
Additional Photography:
Charlie Staniland, Simon Wharton
Proof Reading: *Chris Brierley*
Floral Designs: *Darling Buds of Baslow*
Painting 'Fishermans Cottages': *Ron Davidson*

First published in 2007 on behalf of:
Andrew & Janet Coghlan
Coghlans Cookery School,
www.cookingexpert.co.uk,
www.barrelsandbottles.co.uk,

Regional Magazine Company Limited
RMC House, Broadfield Court, Sheffield S8 0XF
Tel: 0114 250 6300 www.regionalmagazine.co.uk

REGIONAL MAGAZINE COMPANY

Contents

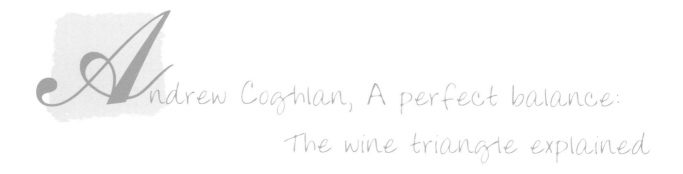

Andrew Coghlan, A perfect balance: The wine triangle explained

The Triangle method is a simple and effective way to illustrate the benefits of "matching" wine and food. It simply breaks down the component parts of each dish and assesses them on the basis of fruit, acidity and tannin which are the three most important aspects of taste. I always try to harmonise the flavours on the palate by using the wine as a contrast rather than a match.

In fact, the term wine and food matching is a misnomer, as we are really trying to find a wine and food contrast, using the wine as an ingredient in the overall dish and finding a flavour balance.

Foods which are high in tannin and acidity, such as salad of forest mushrooms with a balsamic dressing need the balancing of a wine which has a concentrated fruit. Similarly foods which have higher sweetness and tannin content need the acidity in a wine to rebalance the taste scale, such as contrasting a wood-aged Sauvignon Blanc with a sweet young wild salmon fillet served simply with a citrus butter sauce.

This is obviously a very simplistic view, but one which really works on a practical level. Use your judgement to assess the balance of food flavours and then use their position in the triangle to allow the wine to directly contrast. Bear in mind your own personal tastes and you should get some really good contrasts on the palate. Don't take it to the extremes as obviously you can not match a very sweet dessert with a very dry wine.

Typical faux pas include matching oily fish with chardonnay which lacks the acidity balance. If we take an example of smoked salmon with capers, we have a slight tannin with the oak used for smoking the salmon and an oily texture from the fish, minimal tannin content, and some acidity depending on the dressing which is used.

"I always try to harmonise
the flavours on the palate
by using the wine as a contrast
rather than a match."

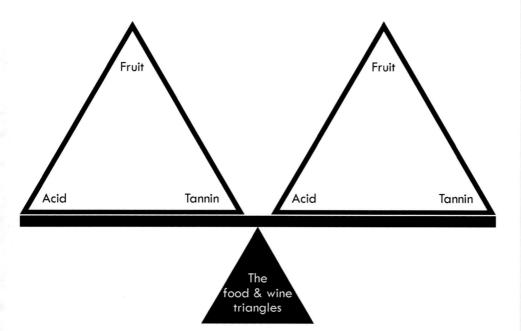

The
food & wine
triangles

I am looking for a wine with medium-high acidity to balance against the fattiness, a high fruit content to harmonise the texture of the tannin in the food and a low tannin content as we already have this in the food.

The best grape variety for this would be Sauvignon Blanc which is all about the fruit and acidity balance. The best choice would be one that has been aged in steel, rather than oak, to keep the tannin down and one with good citrus secondary flavours to ensure acidity is maximised.

I could choose either a Loire Valley Sauvignon, or what is known as a "summer-styled" Sauvignon from the South Island of New Zealand. The Marlborough wines in particular are zippy and fresh, whereas the Hawkes Bay Sauvignons from the North Island are known as winter Sauvignons as they tend to rely on a little oak aging to add depth and colour.

So we embark on this joyful experience of trying to find the perfect balance, the perfect harmony of food and wine, one of life's great pleasures and privileges.

I hope that this book will illustrate my take on this and that you too will enjoy the journey!

Andrew Coghlan

Barrels and Bottles.

- Sent by his father at the age of 14 to the Queen's Hotel, Barnsley, for the summer to knock out of his head the idea that he wanted a career in the hotel industry.
- Despite been given the worst jobs it didn't work – he started "hotel sitting" at the Manor Hotel, Dronfield, Derbyshire, on Sunday evenings while the owners enjoyed a night off.
- Relief manager of the Riverside Hotel, Ashford-in-the-Water, in the Peak District, Derbyshire.
- Completed a four year degree in Hotel Management at Leeds Polytechnic.
- Joined the St George Hotel, Harrogate, as trainee manager, following in the footsteps of Marco Pierre White.
- Assistant manger for Swallow Hotels at Harrogate while still finishing degree.
- Became beverage manager at Hilton International in Mainz, Germany, responsible for bars and Rheingoldhalle, the largest banqueting hall in Germany with 3000 covers.
- Deputy manager at the Royal County Hotel, Durham.
- Deputy general manager, Swallow Hotel, Gateshead.
- Food and beverage manager, AA & RAC five star Swallow Hotel, Birmingham creating a wine cellar fitting of a five star hotel.
- Established his own business with his wife Janet, Barrels and Bottles, Sheffield, as an offshoot of Wine Schoppen, opened in the 1970s by Anne & Eddie Coghlan.
- Bought The Manor House, Dronfield, Derbyshire with wife Janet.
- Contributor to BBC Radio Sheffield food & drink programme since 1994.
- Established Coghlans Cookery School with Janet to run alongside Barrels and Bottles.

Yarra Valley, Australia
Photo Australian Wine & Brandy Corporation

Coghlans Cookery School, Derbyshire

Coghlans Cookery School, Derbyshire, England: Janet's story

I was brought up in the North East of England at a time when handing down kitchen skills from grandparent to parent to child was as normal as the family sitting down together to eat around the dinner table.

Learning to cook was hardly a chore – it was something that young girls like me were expected to do and it became a part of my daily life from an early age.

I picked up a huge repertoire of basic cooking skills from my mother, Ellen Davidson, and grandmother Margaret Wilkinson, who taught me how to make the best use of fresh, local, best quality produce.

It seemed a natural step for me to go to catering college to further my handed-down skills. There I honed my cooking techniques and acquired a sound theory of the essential front-of-house and reception skills required to enter the hotelier's complex world.

But there is nothing like real experience and I was thrilled when I secured a position at the renowned Turnberry Hotel in Ayrshire, Scotland. In the mid 1980s Turnberry was very formal and very old fashioned. But quality ran throughout and it provided a fantastic learning experience.

I found myself working in the room service department, often tending to the suites of some very well known people. There I learned those exacting five star standards that I believe are my hallmark today.

I met Andrew when we were working in a hotel in the North East. By chance, we were both independently offered jobs setting up a new Five Star Swallow Hotel in Birmingham which we both accepted.

A year later we were married and the time had come to launch our own business in Sheffield. We established an offshoot of Sheffield-based Wine Schoppen, the successful business run by Andrew's parents, Eddie and Anne Coghlan.

Our wine business, Barrels and Bottles, went from strength to strength and soon we needed outside catering to help entertain clients in our cellars.

Coghlans catering business was born and remains with us today. It's a match made in heaven – Andrew has continued to develop an extensive knowledge of wine and I have been able to put my catering skills to good use.

Today, our premises in Chesterfield are home to the wine business, run by Andrew and our knowledgeable staff. I have Coghlans Cookery School, ably assisted by head chef and good friend, Simon Lilley.

"Here I am able to stand firm to my beliefs and pass them down to aspiring amateur chefs. I passionately believe that young people should be taught how to cook by the older members of their families, and also at school."

Janet Coghlan

Coghlans Cookery School.

- City and guilds qualification from Monkwearmouth College, Sunderland.
- HCIMA qualification from Newcastle College.
- Food service and restaurant front of house, at the Westin Turnberry Resort, Scotland.
- Trainee manager, Lumley Castle Hotel, Co Durham.
- Reception, Swallow Hotel, Newcastle and Gateshead.
- Reception manager, AA and RAC Five Star Swallow Hotel Birmingham.
- Set up Barrels and Bottles with Andrew in Sheffield.
- Established Barrels and Bottles' successful outside catering business.
- Bought the Manor House Hotel, Dronfield, Derbyshire with Andrew, running the kitchen with head chef Simon Lilley.
- Opened Coghlans School of Wine, Food and Dining at Millthorpe, Derbyshire, teaching cooking skills, an open kitchen and private dining home.
- Relocated to Chesterfield, Derbyshire, with the two businesses, Coghlans Cookery School and Barrels and Bottles sharing the premises.
- WSET Level 2 professional certificate.
- Member of the Institute of Hospitality.

Here I am able to stand firm to my beliefs and pass them down to aspiring amateur chefs. I passionately believe that young people should be taught how to cook by the older members of their families, and also at school.

These days that is a culture that has in many ways departed from our shores and we find ourselves with generations of people who can't cook at all and as a result they eat poorly.

At Coghlans Cookery School I attempt to address those shortcomings. I often find myself teaching some reasonably accomplished amateur cooks who want to improve their skills. But for me the ideal student is one that has none of the basic kitchen skills at all.

Whatever their requirements, I try and instil my students with the beliefs that I have gained from years working with the best people in the business.

The dinner menu that Simon and I present to you here sums up our philosophy. That is: "Add the little extra passion that turns cookery and service from four star to five star; don't cut any corners; seek out and use the finest ingredients; set the table correctly with fresh linen and Sheffield silver; make sure nothing is out of place and above all present something that will give your guests a dining experience to remember."

Coghlans Cookery School

The Menu:

Salmon Four Ways

A tasting of Derbyshire Lamb

White chocolate and
Yorkshire rhubarb mousse
with ginger sorbet

Salmon Four Ways (Serves four)

for the beetroot cured salmon

800g	side of salmon, pin boned, skin on		380g	apple (dessert)
850g	beetroot, peeled		4 tbsp	rock salt
250g	celery		50ml	lemon juice

Blitz in a food processor all the ingredients apart from the salmon (this might have to be done in 2-3 batches).

Place the salmon on a large metal tray, skin side down, place the beetroot curing mixture on top of the salmon and wrap in cling film.

Place in the fridge and place a heavy object on top to weigh down the beetroot. Leave for 36 hours to cure.

for the smoked roast salmon gateaux

100g	smoked roasted salmon		1 dsp	dill
	(from a fishmonger)		2 tbsp	crème fraiche
50g	cucumber			

Flake down the salmon into a bowl, removing any bones and skin.

Finely dice the cucumber removing the seeds first and finely chop the dill.

Add to the salmon and mix together.

Using a pastry cutter 2.5cm diameter, fill with the salmon and then top up with crème fraiche. Smooth over with a palette knife. Carefully remove from cutter and place on a tray until needed.

for the confit of salmon

			1	sprig thyme
150g	salmon, skin on and scaled		1	onion, roughly chopped
300g	duck fat		8	peppercorns
1	star anise		8	juniper berries

Cut salmon into 2cm square pieces, leaving skin on. Place into an ovenproof dish and place in the herbs, spices and vegetables. Add the hot duck fat and cook for 2-3 minutes in the oven.

Remove from the fat and drain on kitchen paper.

Serve on rocket which has been wilted in a hot pan for 30 seconds.

for the fresh and smoked salmon terrine

150-200g	smoked salmon		2	leaves gelatine
100g	fresh salmon		170g	whipping cream
50g	fish stock			salt & pepper

Line a small terrine mould with slices of smoked salmon, with extra to overlap.

Place salmon and stock in a pan and heat up to cook the salmon. Soak gelatine in cold water for 3-4 minutes.

Add the pre-soaked gelatine to the salmon and stock and stir in.

Liquidise the mixture to a purée, pour into a bowl and leave to cool.

Whip the cream to soft peaks and fold into the cooled purée. Season with salt and pepper. Pour into the prepared mould, fold over the excess smoked salmon. Set in fridge. Slice when set.

To plate up: Place one piece of confit on wilted rocket & balsamic glaze, one slice of beetroot cured salmon rolled up with frisse lettuce on top, one gateaux of smoked roast dill on top, one slice of terrine with a caviar dressing.

A tasting of Derbyshire lamb (Serves four)

for the lamb confit

500g	lamb shoulder	1	sprig rosemary
1	carrot, peeled & chopped	1	star anise
1	onion, peeled & chopped	2	cloves garlic, peeled
2	sprigs thyme	500g	duck fat

Place all the ingredients in an ovenproof dish and cook at 130°C for 3 hours until tender.

for the potato rosti

1	large baking potato	20g	butter
1 dsp	chopped chives	1 dsp	oil

Grate the potato and squeeze out any excess water. Season with salt & pepper. Add chives and mix together.
Heat up a large non stick frying pan. When hot, add the potato and press down to get an even layer.
Cook until golden brown, then turn over and colour the other side.
Remove from pan, cut out 8 circles with a 5cm diameter pastry cutter.

for the onion marmalade

500g	onion, sliced	100ml	balsamic vinegar
1 dsp	nut oil	100ml	white wine
25g	butter	120g	demerara sugar

Place the onions in a pan with oil and butter and cover.
Cook over a low heat until onions are very soft, approx 15-20 minutes.
Add the rest of the ingredients, turn up the heat and cook until the liquid has reduced to a sticky glaze.
Season and leave to cool.

for the rack of lamb & sauce

4x250g	rack of lamb	2	sticks celery
4-5kg	lamb bones	2	sprigs rosemary
2	onions, chopped	5 ltr	water
2	carrots, chopped	300ml	red wine
2	sprigs thyme	1 tbsp	redcurrant jelly

Place the bones and vegetables in the oven to brown (very well done).
Place the browned bones, vegetables, herbs and water in large stock pot.
Bring to boil and skim off any scum from the top. Simmer for 6-8 hours and keep skimming the surface.
Drain off the liquid into a clean pan and reduce down to concentrate flavour, add the red wine, redcurrant jelly and keep reducing, until you have 300-400ml left. Thicken slightly if required and pass through a fine sieve.
Prepare the lamb by removing all the sinew, fat and bones, apart from one rack bone which needs to be cleaned. You should be left with the cannon (eye of the meat) and one rack bone at one end.

Finishing the dish

Flake down the lamb shoulder and mix with the onion marmalade. Place into 4 x 5cm rings, with a rosti on the bottom and top to make a little 'gateaux'. Warm up in oven.
Seal the cannon of lamb in a hot pan and cook for 8-10 minutes at 200°C, until pink. Remove and rest.
Warm up the sauce.
In a pan, warm up peeled broad beans and haricot beans.
Place confit gateaux in middle of plate, slice the cannon into four and place on top. Scatter the beans around the plate and sauce around the gateaux.

White chocolate and
Yorkshire rhubarb mousse with ginger sorbet

for the mousse

3 sticks	rhubarb		200g	water
200g	sugar		1	egg yolk
1 tbsp	white wine		125g	white chocolate
1 leaf	gelatine (soaked in cold water)		250ml	whipping cream

Boil the sugar and water together to make a syrup.
Cut the rhubarb the same height as the moulds (4 moulds required approx 5-6cm high, 3cm diameter)
Then cut the rhubarb pieces into thin slices across the length and place in warm stock syrup for 45 minutes-1 hour.
Line the inside of the mould with acetate then line the mould with slices of rhubarb all the way round and place on a tray.
Place the egg yolk in a bowl with wine and whisk over simmering water until pale and thick (not scrambled).
Add the pre-soaked gelatine and whisk in, then add the white chocolate and mix to a smooth consistency. Leave to cool, then add soft peak cream, fold in and pipe into moulds.
Set in fridge for 2-3 hours. Remove from mould and remove acetate.

for the ginger sorbet

275g	caster sugar		400g	ginger ale
50g	fresh ginger, peeled		1	juice of lemon

Bring to the boil the sugar, fresh ginger and half of the ginger ale then simmer for 15 minutes.
Remove from the heat and add the rest of the ginger ale and lemon juice.
Place in a ice cream machine and churn until frozen (without a machine, place in a container and put in freezer and whisk every 30 minutes until frozen).

for the tuile biscuit

85g	butter		85g	icing sugar
90g	egg whites		85g	plain flour

Cream the butter and sugar in a large bowl.
Add the egg whites and flour and mix to a smooth paste. Chill for 1 hour.
Spread a small amount on a non-stick, silicone mat.
Place on a tray and cook for 8-10 minutes at 170°C in the oven.
Remove and shape while still hot.
Store in an airtight container.

Highfield
MARLBOROUGH
SAUVIGNON BLANC
2006

13.0% Vol

750ml

WINE OF NEW ZEALAND

Pictured at Barrels & Bottles, Derbyshire

Andrew's Choice of wines: Coghlans Cookery School

When I looked at the dishes that we had created for our own chapter I wanted to use both wines which went extremely well with the food within my triangle method, but also that reflected the background of the wines that we have worked with for the past 30 years as importers.

The salmon dish has a variety of flavours all based around the sweet and textured feel of the salmon, tempered with the beetroot cure, the sharp acidity of the dressing and also the savoury biscuit tuille which adds yet another texture with the bitterness of the onion seed on the tuille.

I wanted a wine which was fresh and grapey, high in acidity to balance against the sweet fatty texture of the salmon, yet with a distinct fruit character to lift the overall flavour.

I have selected the Highfield Estate Sauvignon Blanc 2006 from Marlborough in New Zealand. Here the Sauvignon Blanc grape variety ripens perfectly and is well suited to the soil of the Marlborough district around the town of Blenheim.

Tasting notes on the 2006 vintage at tasting are as follows;

"Meticulous fruit selection and cold fermentation contribute an abundant spectrum of tropical and herbal aromas. Passion fruit, gooseberry and red pepper fragrances spring from the glass. Extended lees contact adds depth, texture and balance to the palate. The finish is long and crisp.

The aroma really jumps from the glass, giving abundant fruit and a delightful extended finish. This really is a wine match made in heaven and impressed on our filming of series three of Ladette to Lady. I really was most impressed when one of the ladettes selected the Highfield Estate to go with a crab starter. "A real winner" was how it was described.

For the main course I selected a wine from Chile:

Casa Lapostolle Cuvée Alexandre Merlot from Colchagua Valley, a stunning example of Merlot from a multi award winning winery.

The main course flavours are dominated by the richness of the lamb, the savoury stock sauce giving an oily mouth feel which needs soft mature tannins in the balance. This merlot is amongst the best in the world, reduced yield offering intense fruit, ripe tannins and a good but firm acidity.

The wine is produced from 60 year old non-irrigated vines, so they have to fight for their nutrients. The result is a robust style of Merlot with an elegant smooth tannic finish.

"This merlot is amongst the best in the world, reduced yield offering intense fruit, ripe tannins and a good but firm acidity"

Wine List:

Highfield Estate Sauvignon Blanc 2006

Casa Lapostolle Cuvée Alexandre Merlot 2004

Kuhling Gillot Bodenheim Kapelle Riesling Eiswein 1998

Showing the heritage and history of our company, my final choice with dessert is a superb Eiswein from an old established winery in the Rhein area of Germany.

Kuhling Gillot's Bodenheim Kapelle Riesling Eiswein 1998 is quite simply one of the finest dessert wines ever made.

The alcohol level is just 7 percent but the intensity of flavour and aroma comes through with a clarity and precision unmatched by any other sweet wine that I have tasted.

The Eiswein method derives from harvesting the grapes at -9ºC or below, freezing the water in the grape and ensuring that only the fruit extract comes through. The result is bright and intense with equal portions of ripe fruit and crisp cutting acidity that zings on the palate.

This dessert with ripe rhubarb needs that dashing acidity to bring the fruit out of the dish.

Like milling black pepper over fresh English strawberries it brings the fruit flavour out of the dish, the grapey ripeness lingering over the palate for many minutes after the glass is drunk.

Gooseberry and buttermilk sorbet (Serves four)

450g	sugar
600ml	water
6 tbsp	glucose
5 cups	gooseberry purée
3 cups	buttermilk

Make a simple syrup by dissolving the sugar and glucose in the water and then cool.

When cold, add the buttermilk and gooseberry purée to the syrup.

Churn in an ice cream machine until near frozen then remove to the freezer.

Roast rack of Kerry lamb topped with a mosaic of pepper, gently spiced aubergine & basil pesto (serves four)

Rack of Kerry lamb

2	racks of Kerry lamb, (8 bones each)
2 tbsp	olive oil
2 tbsp	Dijon mustard
	salt and black pepper

Aubergine purée

2	aubergines, peeled and roughly chopped
3	finely diced shallots
3	finely diced garlic cloves
1 tsp	chopped fresh rosemary
1 tsp	chopped fresh thyme
3	finely diced red chillies

Mosaic of pepper

1	finely diced red pepper
1	finely diced yellow pepper
1	finely diced green pepper
1 tsp	chopped fresh basil
2	egg yolks
50g	white breadcrumbs

Sun-dried tomato pesto

50g	basil
50g	sun-dried tomatoes
2	cloves garlic, peeled and minced
100g	pine nuts, roasted
100g	Parmesan cheese
50ml	olive oil

Cut the lamb racks in half, so that each portion has 4 ribs, season with salt & pepper. In a medium pan, seal the racks on both sides until golden brown. Remove and place on an oven tray.

To make the crust, mix the diced peppers with the basil, breadcrumbs and egg yolks and combine well.

Coat the lamb with Dijon mustard and then the crumb mix.

Roast the lamb in a preheated oven at 180°C for 15 minutes.

For the pesto put the basil, garlic, pine nuts and Parmesan into a blender and blitz. Slowly pour in the olive oil, which will result in a coarse paste, and add the roughly chopped sun-dried tomatoes.

For the aubergine purée, sauté the garlic, shallots, rosemary, thyme and chillies in a little olive oil for 5-6 minutes. Add the aubergines and season. Continue to cook for 15-20 minutes more over a low heat, remove from the pan and purée in a blender. Check for seasoning and adjust if necessary.

When the lamb is cooked, rest for 5 minutes and then cut in half.

To serve arrange the aubergine purée in the centre of a plate, top with the lamb, and add a liberal drizzle of the sun-dried tomato pesto.

Berries & Bubbles (Serves six)

1kg	mixed soft fruits	a little clear honey
1	small orange, washed	a little Cointreau,
1/2	cinnamon stick	or other fruit based liqueur
225ml	apple juice	

"Select your own combination of fruits for this simple jewel-like dessert, which is full of natural energy. Stoned cherries, blueberries, black or red currants, loganberries, blackberries, strawberries and raspberries are all suitable."

Prepare the fruit according to type : hull and carefully wash berries, and remove cherry stones.

Finely pare the orange; squeeze and strain the juice, then put it into a small pan with the rind, cinnamon stick, apple juice, and honey.

Bring gently to the boil and simmer for 3-4 minutes to infuse the orange rind and cinnamon.

If using cherries, blueberries, currants or loganberries, add them to the hot juices and leave in the liquid to soften as it cools.

When cold, remove the orange rind and cinnamon stick.

Put the fruits and their juices into a serving bowl or individual glasses, along with the softer fruits, and mix gently, adding a little liqueur if you like.

Either serve immediately or chill, as preferred, garnish with mint leaves or other decoration of your choice.

To start it all off I have selected Highfield Estate Riesling from the Marlborough area of New Zealand.

The Park Hotel Kenmare's owners, John and Francis Brennan, have long been supporters of New Zealand wines and John is a great fan of Cloudy Bay, even naming his boat after the wine.

Over the years they have also taken the Highfield Wines, from the early days of when Barrels and Bottles began to import them, and when I was looking for a wine to match the Park's Crab and Watermelon starter, the fresh and lively Riesling was the perfect choice.

The dish requires a fine balance between the sweetness of the crab, the marinated watermelon and the sharpness of the dressing.

This bottle-aged Riesling has great depth of aroma, good firm acidity and a ripe, grapey flavour on the palate.

Perfect summer time drinking!

For the next course I selected Casa Silva Gran Reserva Viognier, from award-winning wine maker Juan Pablo Silva, at the Casa Silva estate in Chile.

I was looking for a wine with structure, as Mark's cauliflower soup and Kenmare smoked salmon has quite punchy flavours – especially the spice from the nutmeg and the oily texture of the Kenmare salmon.

Casa Silva Viognier has everything required to balance the flavours.

The good strong perfume on the nose from this wild grape varietal, seeded originally in the Condrieu area of the Rhône, its satisfying fruit with excellent weight in the glass, and just a hint of tannin from the portion of wine aged in barriques, brings it together perfectly. It's just an excellent harmony.

John & Francis Brennan

With the famous Kerry Lamb I would recommend the wonderful rich and spiced Shiraz from Jorg Gartelmann in the Hunter Valley of Australia.

It is not "over- the- top" as many are from the warm climates of Australia. Jorg uses a cool fermentation method and matures the wine for 13 months in American oak.

The wine has a deep maroon colour, great extraction and ripe blackberry and spiced fruits on the palate. The acidity is cutting, perfect to deal with the fattiness of the lamb and the rich oily texture of Mark's sauce.

The spice and tannins are ripe, so they accept the flavour of the lamb extremely well.

Back to dessert, as mentioned I'm suggesting the Noble Taminga from Tony Murphy made in New South Wales, Australia.

I have selected a wine to go with the main body of flavours, the blueberries, raspberries and strawberries.

Wine List:

Highfield Estate Riesling 2002

Casa Silva Gran Reserva Viognier 2003

Gartelmann Shiraz 2002

Trentham Estate Noble Taminga 2002

The Estate has been producing a Noble Taminga for more than 10 years with the aim of capturing the exotic fruit flavours of this variety.

Unlike many Australian sweet white styles, the Noble Taminga is very much a fruit-driven wine, not dominated by botrytis characteristics or excessive sweetness. It shows excellent fruit and balanced sweetness. The wine displays lifted citrus and apricot aromas with luscious sweetness and balanced acidity.

Taminga is an unusual grape developed by cross breeding three different varieties – Riesling, Farana and Traminer.

It takes a lot of hard work to make this wine, but it has paid off when paired with the finale to a super menu.

John and Francis Brennan are always keen to promote Irish produce and producers. It seems that the Irish way is to keep things in the family and they are so good with it.

The Brennans are superb at investing in people and facilities as well. Stay at the Park, return a year later, and I guarantee the staff will remember your name and where you are from. Now that is hospitality at its very best. Any stay at this hotel is never long enough and always leaves you with a desire to return.

Magnificent Art Deco Ballroom, reopened 1997
The Sheraton Park Lane Hotel, London

The Sheraton Park Lane Hotel, London, England

Surrounded by the buzz of traffic on Piccadilly sits the mighty Sheraton Park Lane Hotel, an Art Deco masterpiece that has entertained many of the world's 'A' list celebrities in its world-famous Ballroom. Built between 1924 and 1927, overlooking Green Park, it is as English as afternoon tea with scones, strawberry jam and Cornish cream.

The magnificent Ballroom re-opened in January 1997, in celebration of the hotel's 70th anniversary, following its complete restoration by owners, Starwood Hotels & Resorts.

Craftsmen from around the world were brought to London to ensure the faithful restoration to its original design. The Ballroom was given back its style using colours true to the Art Deco era – hues of mauve, lilac, purple and pink were used in the fabrics and furnishings.

Throughout its 79 years, The Park Lane Hotel has retained its standing in London and has set the scene for many famous films, from Jeeves and Wooster, Brideshead Revisited, Golden Eye, The House of Elliot to Shanghai Surprise and Mona Lisa.

Such elegance, such splendour – fitting surroundings for our culinary Master who is Andrew Bennett.

Andrew is a classically inspired chef who has followed the time-honoured traditions of some of the world's greatest hotel kitchens. With a CV reading like a culinary route map, it is no surprise that he is now heading one of Britain's leading kitchens with a brigade of 35 eager chefs.

Andrew's goal is simple – to produce restaurant standard food in hotel surroundings, no matter how many covers are served together.

"Our philosophy is to try and match the restaurant experience," he muses. Who would doubt such ambitions from the menu Andrew has provided for us?

The first course was created for the Skills for Chefs conference, a meeting of the best of British chefs. It is very creative and is among guests' favourites at the Park Lane.

Andrew Bennett

**Executive Chef and Food &
Beverage Manager of The
Sheraton Park Lane Hotel.**

· Born in Luton, Bedfordshire,
  trained at Barnfield College,
  completing a two year course
  in City and Guilds.

· Trained for three years at
  Claridges, London, in one of
  the last classical kitchens of
  the day.

· Followed a hugely successful
  career path through some of
  the best hotel and restaurant
  kitchens, including the
  Berkley Portman and Carlton
  Tower Hotels.

· Restaurant experience gained
  with the late Robert Carrier
  and at the Michelin starred
  Rue St Jacques.

· Andrew did his first hotel
  opening for the Conrad in
  Chelsea Harbour.

· The next three years spent at
  the Sopwell House Hotel and
  Country Club in St Albans
  where he gained 2 rosettes.

· Joined the Sheraton Park Lane
  Hotel where he remains
  today after 13 years at the
  helm.

· Saw the hotel come out of
  private ownership and
  become part of the largest
  hotel group in the world
  under the Starwood banner.

· Gained the Craft Guild of
  Chefs Banqueting award in
  2000 and was part of the
  Team UK to gain the gold
  medal for the only
  banqueting competition in
  Toronto.

· Andrew's judging exploits
  have taken him to Dubai and
  he was chairman of judges
  for the Chef of the Year
  competition at the restaurant
  show in 2006.

· A member of the Academy
  for Culinary Arts.

· WSET Level 2 professional
  certificate.

Andrew said: "King crab is a fantastic product. It is a great talking point, a very summery dish which people really enjoy. They do not expect to see it in a banquet for 400 people, but this is the Park Lane Hotel.

"Combining differing culinary skills it is a difficult dish to master, but it's achievable with patience."

The Park Lane's venison comes from Denham Estate and it is a superb product.

As Andrew says, it is versatile, and people are often pleasantly surprised by the quality of the meat. Marinating overnight gives added flavour.

The dessert is another Park Lane popular classic, and again it is a bit of a test of chefs' abilities.

It is very refreshing as it cleanses the palate and there is biscuit to give it crunch and adds to a good contrast of textures. It finishes off this menu particulary well.

The key to Andrew's success is that he doesn't overcomplicate things. He uses just a few elements in each dish, letting the best fresh ingredients do the work.

Longueville Manor, Jersey
Chef Andrew Baird

The Menu:

Hand dived local scallops
with sweet red pepper, garlic
and squid ink velouté

Line caught red mullet with butternut
squash with langoustine and spiced sauce

Hazelnut sablé with "Jivara" chocolate,
sesame ice cream and a
balsamic reduction

Hand dived local scallops with sweet red pepper, garlic and squid ink velouté

Fish stock

500g	clean white flat fish bones
100ml	white wine
50ml	vermouth
100g	onion
50g	leeks
10g	parsley
10	pepper corns
1	bay leaf
5g	chervil stalks
25g	butter

Simply peel, clean and cut your vegetables to a fairly small rough dice.

Place in a heavy bottom pan and warm with the butter and aromatics. Don't get the ingredients too hot, we simply want to break down the cell walls and release the flavour. Cook for approximately 10-15 minutes.

Add the white wine and vermouth and reduce by half.

Add the washed, chopped fish bones and cover with cold water. Turn up the heat and take the stock to simmering point and cook for a further 30 minutes. Skim away any scum as required.

Once cooked pass through a strainer and use as required.

Store for up to 3 days in a refrigerator.

Chicken stock

1kg	clean fat free chicken bones
150g	onion
100g	celery
100g	leeks
100g	carrots
1	bay leaf
10	pepper corns
2 tbsp	parsley stalks
25g	butter

Peel and chop the vegetables and place in a pan with butter. Heat gently until golden brown.

Add the chicken bones, cover with cold water and bring to simmering point. Skim as required.

Cook for approximately 4 hours. Always making sure the bones are covered with liquid. Once cooked, pass through a sieve.

Place into a clean pan and reduce to half of its original volume. Leave to cool and place in the fridge until needed. Store for up to 3 days.

Squid ink velouté

Buy hand dived scallops if at all possible. Open and clean the scallops, keeping the roe if there are any and what we call the frill or skirt around the edge. This should be cleaned in salt water and used to make the squid ink velouté.

25g	shallot
10g	garlic
10g	parsley stalks
10	scallop frills/skirts
100ml	white wine
100ml	vermouth
1ltr	fish stock
20g	butter
400ml	cream
10g	squid ink *(see footnote)

Peel and chop the garlic and shallots. Warm the butter in a heavy bottomed saucepan and add the shallots, garlic, parsley stalks and scallop frills and gently sweat.

Add the white wine and vermouth, bring to the boil and reduce.

Add the cream and finish with squid ink.

Pass through a sieve and serve.

*Footnote on squid ink

Most so-called "squid ink" actually comes from the cuttle fish, but unless you have experience in preparing squid or cuttle fish, it is an extremely messy operation and the results can be disappointing. If in doubt you can buy it prepared from your fishmonger.

Red pepper sauce

2	red peppers
50g	shallots
100ml	white wine
1	clove of garlic
10ml	cream
10g	butter
10ml	olive oil
500ml	previously prepared chicken stock

Roast the red peppers whole with olive oil and garlic. Cook well until soft but with no colour. 15 minutes at approximately 160°C should be fine.

Peel and de-seed the peppers then roughly chop.

Hazelnut sablé with "Jivara" chocolate, sesame ice cream and a balsamic reduction

Hazelnut sablé

400g	peeled roast hazel nuts
570g	unsalted Jersey butter
225g	sugar
700g	flour
7g	salt
2	vanilla pods
200g	egg yolks

Chop the hazelnuts and mix with the butter, sugar and salt.

Place in a food processor and beat until the mix becomes pale in colour.

Fold in the flour and egg yolks together with the seeds from the vanilla pods.

Place between two sheets of silicone paper and roll out to approximately 3mm thickness.

Place in the refrigerator and chill for 20 minutes.

Cut into rectangular shapes and bake in the oven at 180°C for approximately 8-10 minutes then leave to cool.

Jivara chocolate cream

250g	milk
250g	whipped cream
100g	egg yolks
50g	sugar
250g	chocolate "Valhrona Jivara"

Whisk the egg yolks and sugar until it becomes pale in a mixing bowl.

Heat the milk and cream to 85°C then gently pour onto the egg yolks and sugar mix, slowly mixing until lukewarm.

Warm the chocolate until it just melts and add to the mixture, then leave to cool.

Once cooled, place in the refrigerator in a piping bag ready for use.

Sesame ice cream

1ltr	milk
200g	cream
50g	milk powder
6g	salt
2g	agar agar
150g	egg yolks
120g	sugar
40g	trimoline
25g	natural pectin
150g	sesame seeds

Mix the egg yolks, milk powder, agar agar and sugar until pale in colour.

Heat the milk and cream to 85°C and gently pour over the sugar and egg mixture.

Return to a heavy based saucepan and heat until it coats the back of a spatula.

Add the pectin, trimoline and salt, then pass through a conical strainer.

Add the sesame seeds and leave to cool.

Ideally freeze and pacojet, or churn in a traditional ice cream maker.

Balsamic Reduction – simply reduce the balsamic vinegar over heat until a syrupy consistency is obtained.

Kookaburra in a Vineyard, Australia
Photo Australian Wine & Brandy Corporation

Wine List:

Stormhoek The Siren Sauvignon Blanc
Trentham Estate Viognier 2003
1961 Chateau Sigalas-Rabaud 1er grand
cru classe Sauternes

or

Gartelmann Ambrosia 2004

Now with a special place like Longueville Manor, I feel justified in matching a really stunning dessert wine with the final course, the hazelnut sable with Jivara chocolate, sesame ice cream and balsamic reduction.

Some years ago I stumbled upon a small private cellar in which some of the vintages went back to the early 1900s. In amongst the jewels was a 1927 Nuits St Georges, a 1947 Chateau Lafite and a good number of 1961 Chateau Sigalas-Rabaud 1er grand cru classe Sauternes. I bid a high price, but the wines have been stunning and many are still improving despite their age.

The Sauternes is a vision of colour with amber and golden tones indicating the 40+ years it has spent in bottle, yet the aroma still shows youthful acidity and gives great balance, not at all just sticky sweet.

It works just beautifully with the sesame ice cream, giving a cutting acidic forepalate yet deeper raisin and ripe botrytis on the back of the palate. This combination will keep the flavour in your mouth for upwards of 10 minutes after you have finished the dessert. Don't rush to the coffee stage too quickly, just savour the flavour.

At £280 per bottle it would have to be a special occasion wine, so I have also matched a more accessible wine from Jorg Gartelmann in the Hunter Valley. The Gartelmann Ambrosia is very much a serious wine, at just under £20 per half bottle, and Jorg brings out a wonderful ripe sweet aroma, again balanced with a zipping acidity which really does cleanse the palate afterwards.

Whichever you choose you will be guaranteed a stunning flavour match with Andrew Baird's fantastic recipes.

Gartelmann

2004
Ambrosia
Hunter Valley
375ml Wine of Australia 9.5% Vol

Turnberry Golf Course with Ailsa Craig in the background

The Westin Turnberry Resort Ayrshire, Scotland

Ailsa Craig…now there's a name to tickle the taste buds of anyone with a love of traditional regional delicacies. The famous, barren rock whose characteristic dome rises sharply from the wild Firth of Clyde, shares a name with one of the finest flavoured tomatoes known to man. It's fitting that this paradise is also the home of one of the world's greatest hotels.

The Westin Turnberry Resort is known for its famous golf course, the home of The Open Championship on many occasions.

Breathtaking views over the rugged coastline and unforgettable scenery remind guests that they are in one of the world's most untamed locations whilst wrapped in the lap of luxury.

Yet it is the highly acclaimed kitchen and restaurants of its garrulous Executive Chef Ralph Porciani that brings us here. Porciani and Turnberry go together like a professional golfer's hand in his Pittard's glove. Sharing the same belief in Scottish heritage, both strive for perfection. Just as no detail is spared in the hotel, Porciani creates dishes that inspire. He prides himself on using only the best fresh local ingredients and creates menus that are simple, yet breathtakingly satisfying in appearance and giving full expression to the natural flavours.

Porciani shares our philosophy. If you have the finest raw materials available on your doorstep, then use them. Don't mask the flavours, nurture and enhance them, creating an unforgettable dining experience. His kitchen is steeped in the time-honoured values which has made Turnberry one of the best dining hotels in the world. Here, the best quality local produce is fashioned into magnificent classical dishes. But there is a twist. Porciani may be inspired by the local Ayrshire produce, but he is also a creative genius in the kitchen and he adapts traditional recipes with a French influenced contemporary feel.

"The Westin Turnberry Resort is one of the
best dining hotels in the world.
Here, the best quality local produce is
fashioned into magnificent classical dishes."

Ralph Porciani

Executive Chef and Food & Beverage Manager of The Westin Turnberry Resort.

· A second generation Scottish Italian, whose family ran fish and chip shops in Dunbarton.

· Started cooking fish in the family shop, aged 11.

· Attended hotel school to study HND in hotel management.

· Completed training at Le Meridien, Piccadilly, and Le Maison Talbooth, Dedham.

· Executive chef at the Craigendarroch Resort in Scotland, achieving both AA and Michelin recognition for The Oaks Restaurant.

· Executive chef at Edinburgh's Balmoral Hotel, aged 26.

· Executive chef at The Four Seasons Regent Hotel (now the Landmark), The Mandarin Oriental Hyde Park and the Grosvenor House Hotel Park Lane, in London.

· Chef patron of Chamberlain's Seafood Restaurant, Leadenhall Market, London.

· Executive chef, food & beverage manager at The Westin Turnberry Resort heading a team of 150 staff.

· A member of the Craft Guild of Chefs and The Academy of Culinary Arts; he is a past UK national and Scottish chef of the year judge and has also worked on judging panels in the USA, and Dubai.

The menu he offers for us here is typical. It shows off the best of Ayrshire seafood and prime Scotch beef, yet the classic dishes have been adapted for the modern palate.

This is the lunch menu that Porciani created in 2006 to celebrate the Hotel's centenary and each has become a Turnberry signature dish.

The first course celebrates the finest Scottish seafood – one of the last untamed food sources. Succulent Scottish langoustines on the plate here were on the seabed just the day before.

Finest certified Scotch beef is used in Porciani's modern adaptation of Escoffier's classic tournedos Rossini – a plump fillet topped with a slice of pan fried foie gras.

Porciani is passionate about Scotch beef which he says is the sweetest in the world.

His supply is hung by his local butcher for a minimum of 28 days before delivery. It arrives, complete with its 'kill tag' certification attached and allowed to relax and dry a little in the fridge. The meat is then rolled 20 times in cling film and rested for a further three days to shape the fillet and tighten its fibres.

On to dessert which is Porciani's version of the medieval classic. Simple, refreshing and uplifting, this is a dish that excites the senses and cleanses the palate.

The Westin Turnberry Resort
Chef Ralph Porciani

The Menu:

Grilled Scottish Langoustine Niçoise

Tournedos of Scotch Beef Rossini

Lemon Posset with raspberry sorbet,
wild berries and a vanilla shortbread

Grilled Scottish langoustine niçoise (Serves four)

200g	new potatoes		10g	butter
20g	mixed Asian cress		12tsp	dill
12	langoustine tails		5ml	reduced balsamic vinegar
20g	frisée lettuce		12tsp	chervil
30g	pitted black olives		20g	sea salt
10ml	citronette (lemon dressing)		12tsp	basil leaves
20g	French beans		20g	caster sugar
10g	garlic mayonnaise		12tsp	mint leaves
20g	shallots		5g	minced garlic
6	large vine cherry tomatoes		10g	chopped parsley
2	hard boiled eggs		100ml	olive oil
2	fresh anchovy fillets		1	lemon juiced and zested
12tsp	tarragon			

'This is the best way, I feel, to use fresh langoustine from the Ayrshire coast. You will need to prepare the tomatoes 2 hours in advance.'

Oven dried tomato – halve the tomatoes top to tail, lay on a wire rack cut side facing up. Sprinkle with olive oil, chopped parsley, garlic, sugar and sea salt. Dry slowly in a moderate oven for 2 hours.

Salad base – boil whole new potatoes in salted water until tender, cool then peel and slice, cut into round discs with a small fluted cutter, soak for 4 hours in lemon juice, olive oil and lemon zest. Top and tail the beans, blanche in boiling salted water, refresh, then slice into small rounds. Finely dice the black olives, shallots and anchovy.

Niçoise mix – toss the beans, black olives, anchovy and shallot together. Separate the egg yolk from the white and grate the hardened yolk on a fine grater. Add the egg to the Niçoise base. Pick the salad leaves, cress and herbs and place in a bowl.

Langoustine – remove the heads from the tails, lay the langoustine tails flat on a tray and set in the freezer for 30 minutes. This allows the flesh to be peeled out of the shell in one piece. Season with salt, dip into melted butter and grill for 45 seconds-1 minute.

To build the salad – remove the potato from the oil and lemon. Season three slices per plate in a little salt and pepper. Place evenly onto the plate, top with a little garlic mayonnaise, followed with a piece of sun dried tomato. Top with a little more garlic mayonnaise; lay a warm langoustine tail over each tomato. Sprinkle half the Niçoise base around the outside of the potato and dress the other half in some citronette, spoon over the langoustines and top with dressed salad leaves. Finish the plate with reduced or aged balsamic vinegar.

Tournedos of Scotch beef Rossini (Serves four)

4x170g	fillet of Scotch beef	200g	potatoes
10g	black truffle	4tsp	chervil
4x40g	slices of goose or duck liver	200ml	double cream
70ml	Madeira wine	250ml	veal stock reduction
70g	spinach	15g	garlic
40ml	truffle juice	70ml	red wine
300g	celeriac	30g	chopped shallots
100g	butter		

'You need to prepare this dish well in advance, resting the meat for 2 days, freezing the foie gras and soaking the celeriac rave overnight.'

Celeriac dauphinoise – wash and peel the celeriac and potatoes, slice thinly and layer in a roasting tin seasoning with salt and ground pepper as you layer. Finely chop the garlic and place in a pot with the cream; simmer gently for 20 minutes, season with salt and pepper. Pass through a fine sieve and pour over the celeriac and potato, bake in a hot oven until tender. Cool for 30 minutes and then place a weight on top and cool in the fridge. When cold cut into the desired shape.

Spinach – remove all the stalks from the spinach, wash well and dry. Melt some butter in a pan and sauté the spinach gently without colour, season with salt and pepper, drain on some kitchen paper before cooking.

Sauce – sweat the shallots in butter, add the red wine and reduce by half. Pass through a sieve, add the Madeira, truffle juice, chopped truffle and simmer gently, finish with a knob of butter.

Celeriac rave – peel the celeriac, slice thinly and cut into julienne, (fine strips). Soak overnight in lemon juice and water. To cook, drain well and dry on a cloth, deep fry at 200°C until golden brown. Drain on kitchen paper and season with salt.

Foie Gras – slice the foie gras thinly and freeze. When ready to serve season with salt and cayenne pepper, place in a luke warm pan and place on a high heat, cook on each side until evenly caramelised. Drain on kitchen paper before serving.

Beef – use as well hung a piece of fillet as possible (28-30 days). Roll tightly in cling film and rest for two days. Cut into steaks with the cling film around the outside. Season with salt and pepper and sear in a hot pan, allow to rest for 1 minute before removing the cling film, now sear the outside of the beef and cook to the desired cooking degree. For rare meat cook for 12 minutes, medium 17 minutes.

To Serve – place the celeriac and potato in the centre of the plate, surround with the spinach, top with the beef. Napé over the jus, top with celeriac rave, seared foie gras and chervil.

Lemon posset

Pernod jelly

150ml	white wine
100ml	Pernod
15g	gelatine leaves
30g	sugar
100ml	Sambuca

Add the white wine, Pernod, Sambuca and sugar into a heavy based pan.
Heat up and just before it starts to boil take it off the heat and add the pre-soaked gelatine leaves.
Fill the glasses and allow to cool.

Lemon posset

850ml	whipped cream
115g	granulated sugar
3 lg	lemons, juice and zest
100g	white chocolate

Bring the cream, sugar and lemon zest to the boil.
When boiled take it off the stove and add the lemon juice and the white chocolate and stir.
Strain the mixture into a bowl and let it cool in iced water until it is at room temperature.
When cooled fill the glasses containing the jelly with the posset and put it in the fridge to set for approximately 3 hours.

Raspberry sorbet

250ml	water
150g	granulated sugar
23g	glucose
250g	raspberry purée
250ml	cold water

Bring the water, sugar and glucose to the boil and then let it cool.
Add the raspberry purée and the cold water then freeze in an ice cream machine.

Shortbread

160g	unsalted butter
84g	icing sugar
54g	cornflour
188g	soft flour

Whisk the butter and sugar until white and fluffy.
Add the cornflour and flour and mix well.
Cool the dough in the fridge and roll down to 3mm thickness then cut to 2cm x 10cm strips.
Bake at 150ºC for approximately 15 minutes.

Berry compote

100g	blueberries
100g	raspberries
100g	blackberries
200g	caster sugar
20g	cornflour

Heat up the berries with the sugar.
Strain the mixture and take the juice and add the cornflour into the juice.
Cream the juice and add the berries.
Allow to cool.

Wine List:

Tamanis Sauvignon 2005

Chateau Haut Brion 1983 1er Grand Cru Classe Pessac Leognan

Brachetto from Portacomaro d'Asti

For dessert I was a little perplexed at first. I had the lemon and ripe fruit of the Posset, the added fragrance of Pernod, and the ripe Berry Compote to accompany. This was a wild bunch of flavours, which I could not see marrying well with a dessert wine.

After tasting the dish I just knew the wine instantly. Brachetto from Portacomaro d'Asti, made from the Charmat process and giving lush fruit without the depth of strong alcohol.

This wine is only seven percent by volume and as such the flavours that come through are the sweetness of the fruit, the grapes having only been partially fermented. This avoids the clash of the Pernod in the dish, allowing the fruit flavour to cleanse the palate whilst the Pernod hits the gullet section with a little kick on the finish. I particularly like this combination, especially after a heavyweight combination on the main course.

Ralph Porciani is passionate about his food, his background and his family. The Brachetto is a delicious combination of his very best attributes, (although I would never call Ralph sweet); the acid tartness of the lemon, the rich texture of the berries and the honeyed finish of the Brachetto wine.

Alternative dessert wine might include a Riesling Auslese from the Mosel Valley.

Fisherman's Cottages at Whitburn,
adjacent to Latimers Shellfish Deli

The best of British
local food from the regions

There is no shortage of what we would describe as "food heroes" in Great Britain and Ireland – people who demand quality produce and go about what they do with great passion. From our base in the centre of England we are lucky to be able to do business with some of the best. As suppliers to our cookery school, or customers of our wine business, we have met many specialists who inspired us and shared the same philosophy as ourselves.

Like all the chefs featured in these pages, many have become our good friends.

This chapter is a celebration of what is great about the art of gathering nature's gifts to mankind and fashioning them into gastronomic delights.

We focus on a man who harvests one of nature's last wild food resources – the delicious fish and shellfish that can be found off our shores.

There's a former butcher, who for the last 25 years, has turned a small restaurant into one of the most celebrated inns and gourmet dining destinations in the country, championing the very best of his regional produce. He's a stickler for quality and as a result his Lancashire inn, brasserie and banqueting venue has won many regional and national awards.

Finally we showcase a perfectionist who works wonders with chocolate, that rich delicacy that for many a diner has no equal.

In their individual ways these three demonstrate that Britain is up there with the best culinary traditions in the world.

The Fence Gate Inn, Lancashire

Fence Gate Inn
the champion sausage maker

When you have been a butcher for 25 years you have to know your sausages. Especially if you live and work in Lancashire… Luckily for the customers of the illustrious Fence Gate Inn, Kevin Berkins is such a man.

He has been landlord of the award-winning inn at Fence, near Burnley, for 25 years, yet he still makes his own sausages and black pudding, and bones out joints for his famous Sunday lunches.

His devotion to perfection was seen as soon as he took over the premises in 1982.

At that time it was a small restaurant, but Kevin had seen in it a potential that would have passed most people by. He set about the three storey building, originally a 17th Century home to local squires, with vigour. It was extensively modernised and turned into an inn with a charming public bar.

That was only the start. He added two banqueting suites, the Cromdale Room and Patio Suite to accommodate a total of 400 guests. Popular throughout the area, they host weddings, charity balls, society dinners and gourmet clubs. Then came the 104 seater Topiary Brasserie, renowned for it uncompromising standards of food and service.

Kevin is passionate about real food and insists on using as much local produce as possible. He is a keen supporter of the "Dug this Morning" campaign using fresh vegetables from local farmers.

Kevin Berkins & Spencer Burge

He has been well rewarded. His menus have tickled the tastebuds of local people as well as food critics from afar. Recognition has come from Michelin, among many others. In 2007 the Fence Gate Inn was voted winner of the "Best Sunday Lunch" category in the Observer Food Monthly.

Kevin is also proud to be the Lancashire and National BPEX Cat 4 Sausage Champion, employing the fantastic Samlesbury organic pork. The sausages have very high meat content and are made by Kevin from old recipes that he's adapted.

His fame spread from the Fence Gate Inn to Cumbria when he won the Cumberland sausage and 5 counties awards at the North West Fine Food Awards. It was the first time the title had been taken outside the county.

In 2007 Kevin also snatched "The Oscars" of the pub industry, The Publican Free House of the Year.

His recipes here showcase the very best of Lancashire regional produce, having been awarded local food champion 2006/07 and 'Dessert Pub of the Year' 2007.

They include one using Kevin's signature Samlesbury pork sausages, layered with his homemade black pudding, smoked bacon, potatoes from Southport are topped with Mrs Kirkham's smoked Lancashire cheese.

We also demonstrate the remarkable strength of the North West's wide variety of local produce with another starter called A Taste of Lancashire, based on the region's seafood, an unusal dish pairing Lancashire cheese and apple and finally, the Fence Gate Inn Cheese slate offering four of the region's finest.

Food made in heaven – a perfect challenge for our wine matching skills.

Taste of Lancashire

300g	shortcrust pastry		for the beurre mania	
2	leeks		4oz	flour
1	side Lancaster smoked haddock		4oz	butter
20g	Mrs Kirkham's smoked Lancashire cheese			
	a pinch of chopped chives			
	salt & pepper			

Line a 2 1/2 inch case with short crust pastry and blind bake at 180°C for 12-15 minutes.

Seal with egg wash and bake for a further minute.

Sauté leeks in a pan with a little butter without colouring then season, evenly distribute between tart cases.

Poach 1 side of smoked haddock in milk until cooked and tender, about 8-10 minutes. Remove from milk keeping liquid.

Rub together equal quantities of flour and butter to create Beurre Mania. Stir into the milk over heat until slightly thickened (consistency of anglaise).

Flake the smoked haddock on top of the leeks and cover with a dessert spoon of the sauce.

Top with grated smoked Lancashire cheese and chopped chives.

for the Shrimp
6	crostinis
50g	garlic butter
180g	Morecambe bay shrimp

Warm through garlic butter being careful not to heat too much.

Add the shrimp to the butter and remove from heat. Stir until all of the shrimp are coated in garlic butter. It is important not to overcook the shrimp or they will become tough.

Arrange shrimp on crostini's to serve.

for the Smoked Salmon
1/2	cucumber
12	pieces smoked salmon
30	small caper berries

Cut all of the black fat from the salmon and form a rose by wrapping the two pieces around your thumb.
Peel cucumber and thinly slice.
Arrange on a plate with caper berries and place the salmon on top of the cucumber.
Garnish with a sprig of thyme.

Lancashire Tart

250g	Lancastrian or Cumberland sausage	1/4	pint cream
670g	black pudding	5	eggs
10	slices smoked bacon	500g	Mrs Kirkham's smoked Lancashire cheese
2	large potatoes, peeled		chopped parsley
1	pint milk		salt & pepper

Cook the sausage and bacon and allow to cool. Trim fat off bacon.

Slice the potatoes to approximately 4mm in depth and steam until just cooked (if a steamer is not available simply boil).

Thinly slice the black pudding and sausage being careful to slice evenly as this will affect the overall appearance of the tart.

Line a 12 inch by 1 1/4 inch tart case with short crust pastry and blind bake at 180°C for 15-20 minutes.

Seal with egg wash and bake for a further minute.

Mix milk, cream and eggs, beat slightly and lightly season.

Now the ingredients are ready to assemble start by placing black pudding in the bottom of the tart then a ladle of cream mix, a sprinkle of smoked Lancashire cheese and a pinch of parsley.

This process is repeated with the sausage, then bacon, then sliced potato and finally by sprinkling chopped parsley and smoked Lancashire cheese on top.

This is then baked for 40 minutes at 140°C until the liquid is set.

When cooling place a weight on top of the tart to compress the layers.

Portion as you would like but this will provide 14 portions as a starter size.

Chef's Tip

It is important not to overlap ingredients when building your tart and sprinkle cheese between each layer as this helps the tart to keep its shape when portioned and although we use the cream mix to set each layer this is not a quiche so do not put too much liquid in your tart, simply enough to set the ingredients in place when pressed.

Individual Lancashire Apple Tart

for the sweet pastry		12oz	sugar
3lb	flour	6	eggs
1 1/2lb	butter	2tsp	vanilla extract

Beat the sugar and eggs together with a hand whisk only until sugar starts to dissolve, do not beat until light and fluffy.
Add butter, do not cream.
Add the vanilla extract and finally flour until if forms a smooth paste.
Roll into cylinders and leave to rest in cool room.
Mould into a case and bake at 180°C for 15 minutes.

for the apple compote		for the ice cream
2lb	Bramley apples peeled, cored and chopped into small pieces	1 ball Huntley Farm ice cream
100ml	white wine	
300g	sugar	

for the apple crisps			
1	Golden Delicious apple, thinly sliced on slicer	300ml	water
1	juiced lemon		icing sugar to dust

Dip apple slices in water with the juice of one lemon and lay onto greaseproof paper with icing sugar dusted on.
Dust sugar over top and place in oven at 50°C to dry out.

Put small amount of creamy Lancashire cheese in the bottom of the pastry case followed by some apple compote then top with more cheese.
Place in the oven for 10 minutes at 170°C until the compote is hot and the cheese has melted.
Arrange apple crisps on top of tart and carefully place a ball of vanilla ice cream on top.
Finish with another apple crisp.

SOFT ORGANIC
BLACK STI
BLUE
MRS KIRKHAM'S
SMOKED
BLACK BEAUTY
BOMB

Lancashire Cheese Slate

Black Sticks Blue
Made by Butlers of Inglewhite

We chose this over many Lancashire Blues as we feel this is the best by far, being creamy with a little zip and a very sophisticated bite.

Smoked Creamy Lancashire
Made by Mrs Kirkham of Goosnargh

Lancashire handmade cheese wheels, smoked at Lancaster Smoke House perceived by many to be the best of all smoked cheese. It is also number one in our opinion. A creamy smoked flavour with a true Lancashire texture.

Strong Black Beauty Bomb
Made by Andrew & Pauline Shorrock of Goosnargh

The Black Beauty Bomb is a sixth month matured strong creamy Lancashire in its own black waxed jacket. This is one of my personal favourites. It has creamy texture, depth of flavour but with a bite. Simply stunning.

Organic Soft Lancashire
Made by Leagrams Organic Dairy of Chipping

This cheese is produced only by Leagrams Organic Dairy making it a unique cheese experience. Made in approximately 8oz individual waxed wheels the texture and appearance being as a soft cream cheese, mellow, spongy and gentle on the palate. A young cheese which develops depth of flavour as it ages.

Just like you would match food & wine we have attempted to match cheese & biscuit, here is a selection of approximately 8 biscuits, our recommendations would be:

Black Sticks Blue: a plain biscuit possibly, Carr's Table Water.
Black Beauty Bomb: again a plain biscuit, Walkers Fine Oatcake
Both of these plain biscuits will not detract from the cheese.

Mrs Kirkham's Smoked Lancashire: Poppy Wafer Thins, for good measure also the Charcoal Wafer Thins.
Organic Soft Lancashire: Fudges Sesame Seed and Pumpkin Seed Flatbreads.
Also accompany with 1 plain and 1 sesame seed breadstick.

The Lancashire cheese slate is presented with black and white grapes, strawberries, a small wedge of homemade fruitcake, some apple and fig chutney and butter. For that finishing touch a shot glass filled with an espuma of celery and apple, a recently designed recipe which is an interesting way of incorporating these traditional accompaniments.

Wine Selection

Kevin is a good friend of mine and he knows his wines. His recipes here offer a great platform for some wine matching. There is an awful lot going on in the Taste of Lancashire dish with sweet prawns, smoked flavours from the fish, and the nutty richness of the oil.

I have selected a slightly unusual partner. Sparkling wines are generally limited in use as an aperitif or as a toast to mark a special celebration, yet they have great qualities to go with a variety of flavours and textures during a meal.

Louis Roederer's Quartet from California has won the very top award for sparkling wines, namely the Sparkling Wine Trophy from the International Wine Challenge, beating off many illustrious rivals from Champagne and beyond!

It is a blend of Pinot Noir and Chardonnay from the Anderson Valley, where the warm climate benefits the ripeness of the grapes.

Deep with red fruits on the nose and dark fruits with prominent acidity on the palate gives us a great match to the contrasts of sharpness and sweetness in the dish. Finish the bottle later over coffee and the ripeness of the fruit will still stand the test, a great wine from the Roederer family of vineyards.

Lancashire Tart is another regional dish which really shows the strength of flavours in what we would traditionally call "country" or "peasant" food.

Kevin uses his background as a master butcher to great effect with this Sausage, Black Pudding and... plenty of spice and texture in the Black Pudding requiring a full on spiced and tannic texture in the wine, something with a bit of umph in it!

Gartelmann's Diedrich Shiraz from Australia's Hunter Valley fits the bill.

Shiraz is the oldest Hunter red wine variety, and is the flagship red wine for the region.

This deep maroon wine has an aroma of plum, mulberry and blackberry fruits with pepper and spicy oak.

Its palate shows rich plum and mulberry fruits, wrapped in velvety tannins with a long finish. A perfect balance.

For the Apple Tart I have selected Coteaux du Layon, Chateau La Roulerie, Germaine, from the Loire Valley.

It always amazes me when I find a wine which goes equally well with sweet things as it does with savoury dishes. I still don't really understand how this can be. On the one hand the sweetness of this lush Chenin Blanc offers honey and ripe berries, yet on the other hand it has a bite to the acidity, an elegant mature tannin texture and an unbelievably long finish. Simply put, it works.

The tart, with the smoked Lancashire cheese in the base, and ripe English apples over, offers the best of both worlds. A savoury-sweet tart with a sweet yet savoury wine.

Kevin's delicious Cheese Slate takes me to Madeira for the final wine selection at the Fence Gate Inn.

I have chosen Barbeito Boal 1995 Single Cask whose extraordinary lemoniness when it was first bottled has now been supplemented with nuts, marmalade and a tropical fruit note.

Vinhos Barbeito was set up by Mario Barbeito in 1946 and now Ricardo de Freitas is the third generation to run this small, specialist company. Barbeito no longer uses caramel in any of its Madeiras, making a huge difference to quality. Over the last couple of years, Ricardo has been picking up gongs by the handful for his work, and I foresee many more to come.

Mick Burke
a passion for chocolate

South Yorkshire born Mick Burke was the first lad at his school to have cookery lessons, a feat in itself worthy of special mention. He must have taken a lot of flak in his youth and now he's like one of his finest chocolates – he has a firm exterior concealing a soft centre.

Coghlans Cookery School has a long association with Mick, whose expertise with desserts has made him a bit of a celebrity in cookery circles.

He's also an award winning senior lecturer with a passion for pastry and sugar work which is awe inspiring.

In many ways it's a tough lot being a dessert chef – their work follows other perfect dishes, yet it's down to them to create that lasting good impression.

Mick works with the finest ingredients and in pastry and chocolate work, there has to be absolute precision in quantities and methods.

He says his work is a metamorphosis from science to art, and his recipes are his formulae.

His tools of the trade are top grade chocolate couverture, full fat cream and milk, fresh eggs, butter, sugar, flour and seasonal fruits.

Here he has prepared for us a confection of chocolate and apples – an unusual combination – but it works.

It consists of a chocolate dome, made from chocolate mousse, chocolate sponge and a round of caramelised apple, coated with a couverture glaze. It's decorated with a delicious apple compote and a miniature "toffee apple", a Chinese apple coated in caramel.

Notes